Return to
Peggy Miller
(607) 275-0692

# THE HOUR BETWEEN
# DOG AND WOLF

*[signature: Laure-Anne Bosselaar]*

### Poems by
### Laure-Anne Bosselaar

Foreword by

**Charles Simic**

*For Peggy — for your heart,*
*passion & faith in poetry :*
*my gratitude & friendship,*

*[signature: Laure-Anne]*

**BOA Editions, Ltd. ❦ Rochester, NY ❦ 1997**

*7/98*

LC #: 96–86385
ISBN: 1–880238–47–0 paper

First Edition
97 98 99 00   7 6 5 4 3 2 1

Publications by BOA Editions, Ltd.—
a not-for-profit corporation under section 501 (c) (3)
of the United States Internal Revenue Code—
are made possible with the assistance of grants from
the Literature Program of the New York State Council on the Arts,
and the Literature Program of the National Endowment for the Arts,
the Lannan Foundation,
as well as from the Rochester Area Foundation Community Arts Fund
administered by the Arts & Cultural Council for Greater Rochester,
the County of Monroe, NY,
and from many individual supporters.

Cover Design: Daphne Poulin-Stofer
Cover Painting: "Winter Landscape" by Constant Permeke
Author Photo: Mathieu Ducaroy
Typesetting: Richard Foerster
Manufacturing: McNaughton & Gunn, Lithographers
BOA Logo: Mirko

BOA Editions, Ltd.
A. Poulin, Jr., President
(1938–1996)
260 East Avenue
Rochester, NY 14604

*Light: Mathieu and Maëlle*

*Grace: Kurt*

*and in memory of Al Poulin*

*Sois sage, ô ma Douleur, et tiens-toi plus tranquille*
*Tu réclamais le Soir, il descend; le voici.*

—Charles Baudelaire


*Speak of your heart*
*burned to a seed of ash,*
*and love, a small white stone*
*gleaming in the shallows.*

—John Haines

# CONTENTS

# FOREWORD

A carnival of images is what this delightful book primarily is : A man buys his first cane. Guards mop brains from the jail floor. Jesuits brandish crucifixes. A speck lifted from somewhere lands on the poet's desk. A little boy has a large hole in his tongue. The cow is butchered; the farmer stoops to stroke a child's cheek, his nails framed with blood. On a garage wall there is a sculpture of the Madonna in her white robes. The sea shells glisten in the sink. Black spiders escape into the purple shadow of concord grapes. Newlyweds wave bloodstained sheets from somber windows at dawn.

Poetry is one of the oldest of human activities. The often-made claim is that poetry is on its deathbed, that its last gasps are merely the recapitulations of what has been said thousands of times before, that every style and technique has already been invented, that originality belongs to its past. If American poets as a group tend to think otherwise, if American poetry is the most promising literary enterprise we have going, this must be merely the delusion of our poets. The intellectuals and the academics, the ones who usually argue this way against the relevance of poetry, have one secret: They do not read very much contemporary poetry. They are persuaded by claims that have plausibility only as long as one remains illiterate and incurious as to what is being written today. A poet like Laure-Anne Bosselaar comes along and one knows, even after reading only a few of her poems, that one is in the presence of an original. Never before has one heard anything quite like that, one thinks. It is a wonder of wonders, this ability of poetry to renew itself.

Laure-Anne Bosselaar grew up and spent a good portion of her adult life in the Flemish part of Belgium. As in any first book of poems, many of the poems are autobiographical. They take place in that morally difficult period just after the Second World War when the cities of Europe and people's lives were still in ruins. She is sent as a child to a convent boarding school, and some of the most dramatic and successful poems in the book deal with her experience in that austere and terrifying institution. She had an upbringing, one might say, with alternating moments of cruelty and religious ecstasy. This is the story of devotion, rebellion, sexuality within the walls of an asylum in the midst of a country trying to resume its normal existence after the horrors of the war. Bosselaar has a strong sense of individual destinies. Many of the poems are portraits, studies of eccentric characters, those who find themselves at odds with their surroundings. "Lost souls roaming," she calls them. She is a poet of finely observed detail and sharp psychological insight.

"Why is it that we remember one thing rather than another?" she asks in a poem. We can't say for sure, of course. Still, reading her poems, it occurred to me, that we tend to remember two categories of things:

First there are moments of experience which stand out in their unusual vividness. Then, paradoxically, we also store away experiences that are profoundly ambiguous. The first are mostly visual memories and the latter have to do with our experiences of people and events, experiences that we cannot resolve without betraying their genuine complexity. It is their delicious mixture of clarities and ambiguities that makes them stick in our minds.

If you subscribe to the unconventional notion that the greatest liberty is to be found not far from anarchy, America is any poet's visual heaven and hell, as our poet here realizes. "No ideas, but in things," American poets sing in their cradles. Anyone with a good pair of eyes is welcome to our poetry. Since Whitman, we've been trying to fit the bewildering variety of things we encounter in our American lives into some kind of coherent collage. "The Worlds in This World" is the name of the first poem in this book. An autobiography and an inventory is our common project.

The issue of ambiguity is more complicated. If our experiences could neatly be divided into tragic and comic, life would be much easier to understand. There would be no residue of uncertainties to make us lie sleepless at night. It's the closeness of the tragic and comic, the way they brush lips, so to speak, that makes them memorable. That's what art demands and that's precisely what these poems wrestle with. As Bosselaar says in "White-Out,"

. . . even God could
get lost on a night like this, searching for shelter . . .

If we had nothing but "insomnia's *films noirs*" to contend with, it would be a miserable life. Luckily, we are also given occasional, untroubled moments of intimacy which Bosselaar's many love poems in this book celebrate. In the best lyric tradition, she struggles again and again to find words for:

> . . . their bodies'
> naked blurs: those indefinable hues
> of wrists, thighs, elbows—their tints and shadows . . .

and happily for us, she finds them in poem after poem.

Laure-Anne Bosselaar understands the complexities and the endless contradictions of our contemporary human predicament. Hers is an authentic poetic voice, one serious enough to be heard at the end of this long and brutal century. She writes wise poems about memory, poems whose art lies in their ability to make these memories ours too.

What more could anyone of us ask of poetry?

—Charles Simic

# THE HOUR BETWEEN DOG AND WOLF

⧗

*THE WORLDS IN THIS WORLD*

# The Worlds in This World

*This is the world to love. There is no other.*
—Stephen Dobyns

Doors were left open in heaven again:
drafts wheeze, clouds wrap their ripped pages
around roofs and trees. Like wet flags, shutters
flap and fold. Even light is blown out of town,
its last angles caught in sopped
newspaper wings and billowing plastic—
all this in one American street.
  Elsewhere, somewhere, a tide
recedes, incense is lit, an infant
sucks from a nipple, a grenade
shrieks, a man buys his first cane.
  Think of it: the worlds in this world.

Yesterday, while a Chinese woman took
hours to sew seven silk stitches into a tapestry
started generations ago, guards took only
seconds to mop up a cannibal's brain from the floor
of a Wisconsin jail, while the man who bashed
the killer's head found no place to hide,
and sat sobbing for his mother in a shower stall—
the worlds in this world.

Or say, *one* year—say 1916:
while my grandfather, a prisoner of war
in Holland, sewed perfect, eighteen-buttoned
booties for his wife with the skin of a dead
dog found in a trench, shrapnel slit
Apollinaire's skull, Jesuits brandished
crucifixes in Ouagadougou, and the Parthenon
was already in ruins.

That year, thousands and thousands of Jews
from the Holocaust were already—*were
still*—busy living their lives;
while gnawed by self-doubt, Rilke couldn't
write a line for weeks in Vienna's Victorgasse,
and fishermen drowned off Finnish coasts,
and lovers kissed for the very first time,
while in Kashmir an old woman fell asleep,
her cheek on her good husband's belly.

And all along that year the winds
kept blowing as they do today, above oceans
and steeples, and this one speck of dust
was lifted from somewhere to land exactly
here, on my desk, and will lift again—into
the worlds in this world.

Say now, at this instant:
one thornless rose opens in a blue jar above
that speck, but you—reading this—know
nothing of how it came to flower here, and I
nothing of who bred it, or where, nothing
of my son and daughter's fate, of what grows
in your garden or behind the walls of your chest:
is it longing? Fear? Will it matter?

Listen to that wind, listen to it ranting
   *The doors of heaven never close,
      that's the Curse, that's the Miracle—*

⧗

# The Feather at Breendonck

I am praying again, God—pale God—
here, between white sky and snow, by the larch
I planted last spring, with one branch broken at the elbow.
I pick it up, wave winter away, I do things like that,
call the bluebirds back, throwing yarn and straw
in the meadow, and they do come, so terribly blue,
their strangled *teoo-teoo*

    echoing my prayer *Dieu, Dieu*—
the same *Dieu* who stained the feather I found
in the barbed fields of the Breendonck Concentration Camp
near Antwerp in 1952. My father tried to slap it
out of my hand: *It's filthy.* But I held on to it—
I knew it was an angel's. *They only killed
a few Jews here*, he said, *seven, eight hundred, maybe.*

So I wave their angels away with my feather,
away from my father, away from the terribly blue skies
over the Breendonck Canal, where barges loaded bricks
for Antwerp, where my father loaded ships for Rotterdam,
Bremerhaven and Hamburg—as Antwerp grew,
and the port expanded, and his business
flourished, and all the while he kept repeating:

    *That's all we needed: a good war . . .*

⌛

# The Pallor of Survival

I'm lucky: autumn is flawless today,
sidewalks freckled rust and red, and the sun
gentle. I'll take the back streets
to the bookstore—it's a longer ride—but I avoid
the street where St. John the Evangelist Church
faces that seedy building with a sign flashing
                    *Jews for Jesus*
The last time I pedaled between them I felt
a draft there, something so chilling I gasped.

I don't know what happened to Judith Aaron,
placed in 1945 at the Mater Immaculata convent
in Brussels, after she was repatriated from Bergen-Belzen.
Judith who waited eleven years for some—*any*—
next of kin to claim her. No one ever came
to the black and brass door. And we

never saw her again after she turned eighteen
and left that very morning, still wearing the convent
uniform, but the blouse open three buttons down
and the socks low on her white ankles. She left
on a sleety day in October, years after—
from under a bed in the infirmary—I'd seen

what the nuns did to her when she confessed
she masturbated: bending her over, pulling down
her panties to ram the longest part of an ivory crucifix
into her, hissing: HE is the Only One Who Can Come
Inside You—No One Else—You Hear?

She didn't let out a sound, not a sigh:
the pallor of survival carved into her face
when she pulled her panties up again.
I think she made it: she was of the stone
statues are made from. And yet, I still

search—Judith, I can't stop searching—
for signs we made it,
        you, me and the others,
signs I find in the smallest things:
a flawless sky, a leaf autumn
turns, an open gate.

⌛

# Leek Street

in Bruges, was a cul-de-sac so narrow
cars never scarred its mossy cobblestones.
Every house had a niche above the door
for a Saint, and a little garden framed by high
brick walls. Carved into the back rampart,
an iron gate opened on the Wool Canal.
        Now and then, a muskrat's head
pearled out of that green velvet, then slipped
back into the water. The Belfry rang a bronze
quiver through the drizzle every quarter.

        Yochemke lived at No. 8 in the only house
with open curtains and no Saint.
He was nine, had a large hole in his tongue
and six numbers tattooed on his arm.
They did this to him when he was a baby, he said,
he couldn't remember if it hurt.
I loved him so much I repeated the numbers
inside his arm every night until I fell asleep:
*Yochemke-seven-four-three-two-three-six*
        It rained the day he said I could put
my finger through his tongue.
He shut his pale gray eyes, I shut mine,
and he slowly closed his lips around my finger.
Something guilty and deep made me want to cry.

        We were setting muskrat traps by the canal
the first time he said he loved me. I wanted
to play the piano for him, or have curly hair
and be beautiful, I was so happy.
        The muskrats were for his father
who made collars and muffs out of them
to sell at the Fish Market. He always came
back with something for Yochemke. Once,
it was a glass marble with a heart of green,

blue and gold. When Yochemke gave it to me,
we were sitting by the canal stirring the algae
with willow sticks. His father had told him
the heart of the marble was what the world
looked like before the Germans.

That night, we climbed the Belfry tower
to make the bronze bell ring with the marble.
Up there, looking down at the brown roofs
and fields of the world, we wanted to change it back
to how it was, make it look like the marble again.
We'd set traps for the Germans, poke
holes in their tongues, hurl their bodies in the canal,
and all the muskrats of Bruges would feed on them,
fatten, we'd trap them, and –
*I'll buy you a piano,* said Yochemke,
*we'll be the richest muff makers in Belgium.*
Then, with our marble, we tapped the bell
as hard as we could and listened to its small sound
float out over the canals.

# Amen

I'm not allowed to do it, so I hide behind a curtain,
take a last breath through my mouth, slip my thumb
in the space where my front teeth are missing,
find the vacuum between palate and tongue, and suck.
Slowly at first, then in cadence with the panic
in my chest. My parents are packing again, mother
hastily stuffed my suitcase last night: it's already
downstairs. They are leaving on a big boat, I'll
stay on a farm, somewhere in Flanders.

After a month, I get used to living there,
with the men, the woman, the branch whipping the roof.
I spend my days in the hollowed trunk of a willow, watching
Percherons lash at flies with tails thick and swishing
like mother's shawls. One day, the farmer's wife
wakes me before dawn. The black and white cow
had stillborns during the night. She is hemorrhaging,
they must slaughter her before she dies. I must
help. I run barefoot to the barn.

The air swarms with flies, bare-chested men
swear in the dark. One of them hands me a wooden pail,
orders me to empty it in the ditch. It's full with a warm,
black liquid. I run, choking with the stench and moans,
pail heavy, warm stuff sloshing and splashing.
I throw it in the ditch, run back; they give me
another one, I hurry to the ditch again.
I want to vomit, but don't—I'm needed—I'm
almost happy.

Day lifts. The cow is butchered. Men carry huge cuts
from the barn to the farmhouse. One of them hands me
something fleshy and gray, I hold it to my chest: fingerlike
things stick out of it. It's the udder. I've never seen one
so near before. I go to the willow, hold the udder in my lap.

It's not cold yet, not dead. I try to remember my mother
when she's warm, when she's there. I brush my cheek
against the udder, my lips find a nipple, I suck it in,
slowly at first, then find the cadence, the cadence . . .

When I bring the udder to the woman,
she throws it in a basin, adds onions and turnips,
and puts it on the stove. All afternoon I help her
wash the men's clothes in the stone sink, she sings
when she hangs my nightdress on the line.
At night, when she lifts the udder from the basin,
it has shrunk. She draws a cross on it with her knife
to bless it, slices it, puts the slices to fry.
They curl upwards in the sizzling suet.

I watch her patient face, the men's
strong hands as they hold out their plates.
I'm hungry, tired, sucking my thumb. The farmer
stoops to stroke my cheek, his nails are framed
with blood. He pours dark beer on his slice, chooses
the biggest turnip and hands me his plate. My heart
aches with something new, it's terrible, soothing,
I want to feel this forever. At Grace, his hand is a crown
on my hair. He nods at me when he says *Amen.*

⊠

# Days of Rules

He's like a crow in a crowd of magpies
the old priest who comes to say Mass
at the convent. To reach the chapel, he creeps
into the cloister garth by a rusted gate,
and slips through habits dripping
on clotheslines: six identical rows
of starched nuns, hanging stiff and headless
by the rhododendrons next to the laundry room.

Inside, bare-armed novices with wooden
tongs stand around steaming basins, fishing out
dozens of sanitary napkins. Each has four
loopholed ribbons, fasteners for the black
Bakelite buttons sewn inside our underpants
for *les jours de règles*, the days of rules.
Blessed days: P.E. is forbidden. Cursed days:
washing with warm water is forbidden too.

"It makes blood *flow*," Dorm Sister says,
"only cold *coagulates*." So we wash
with freezing water, always wearing
our washroom uniforms: coarse beige
linen tubes slit on both sides, tied on the shoulders
with frazzled strings. No bath, no shower,
we must stand at the sinks, obey the rules: first
lift the eyes, only then the chemise

and keep the eyes fixed on the third
tile above the metal mirror. Even on warm-
water days, standing three-by-three in curtainless
showers, we never wash without the chemise.
We must undress under them, wash, dry
and put on our underwear under them,
and only then hang the dripping things
on our numbered hooks.

Anne sometimes disobeys the rule, lifts
her chemise too high, too long, cooing to us,
eyes transparent with longing, and shows us
her shivering body and new breasts,
wants us to show ours too—wants us to whisper
        *tits, nipples* . . .
Sundays, when most of the girls have gone home,
Ann and I go to the bleach scented nave

        of the laundry-room rhododendrons:
she coils against me, trembling
to be held so close, chapped hands clenching
my chapped hands. We hide there,
an odd Pietà, while the old crow
drones his way back through the habit maze,
and Bruges hums beyond the walls.

# Little Sisters of Love and Misery

## 1. May Field Trip to Ostend

When the slaughterhouse smoke was no longer blown
inland by the wind, but North, to the sea, and the lapwings
blabbered behind the chapel; when the refectory tables

were freckled with strawberries, and it was no longer dark
at Matins' *Ite Missa Est;* when punishment switched
from praying to weeding the rose garden,

and novices bleached their aprons in the sun—Judith, Marie
and I started counting the days till the first Sunday in May.
That morning, Sister Serena distributed our summer uniforms,

Mother Superior rounded up every one for the Field Trip to Ostend,
and Sister Kelleen tapped the shoulders of three girls
who were to stay behind to help her chafe the Chapel floor.

For the last four years it had been us: we never broke
the silence about the only time she broke hers, never spoke—
even among each other—about what happened those nights,

or wondered why. To this day, I still can't explain. But this
I know: a kind pain breaks in me when I see broken glass,
or wine spilled. A kind pain. We all have a few.


## 2. Sister Kelleen

She was pale, thin, young, tall. Because she was Irish and barely
spoke Flemish, she couldn't teach, and was given the Chapel to keep.
It was said she tended to it in the middle of the night,

walking through the rose-garden as if in daylight, choosing
the lushest rose for St. Bosco. Winters, she folded a different
colored handkerchief at his feet every day, though

no one saw her do it. Or smile, or lift her eyes. But in May,
on Field Trip Day, Sister Kelleen woke from her torpor. It started
with her foot, at breakfast, although with the refectory

bustling with lunch-packing and strawberry eating, I think
no one noticed but me. Like a bird caught in a net, her foot
fluttered, quivered, then jerked under the swart hem of her habit.

The motion crept to her knees, hips, her crucifix swayed, not
sideways but beating her chest. Her hands escaped
from the black corridors of her sleeves, one stilling the crucifix,

the other her knees. Eyes afire, she watched the school
escape in the sun-drunk street in marine-blue rows of three.
Voices stopped echoing from the nunnery walls:

the school was empty but for Judith, Marie, Sister Kelleen
and me. *Mes petites soeurs d'amour et de misère,*
she whispered once: *my little sisters of love and misery . . .*


### 3. Glass-Shard Night

    We followed her, silently, through empty corridors,
dank pantry stairs, through coal and furnace rooms,
to the tiny mass-wine cellar. Empty bottles were piled

on the dirt floor, the full ones—like stiff rows of nuns—
were locked behind the grated doors of an oak cupboard.
Sister Kelleen shut the cellar door, handed us each

a pair of black cotton gloves: *Shards, girls, we need good
sharp shards,* opened the cupboard, snatched a bottle,
pulled out the cork, took a long gulp—

We knew what to do: kneel by the empty bottle pile, slip on the gloves,
grab a bottle by its neck, and wait for the signal. It never took long:
with a wail, her half-empty bottle split the air over our heads

and shattered against the wall. The cellar shook with the cry,
the crash of glass on bricks: it was our turn. We hurled our empty bottles.
From behind us—*More!*—she threw hers, sopping us with claret,

and we screamed, and we shrieked, and bumped into each other,
and she drank and drank, and bottles shattered—*More! More!*—
until a year's worth of masses lay there, smashed on the slushy floor.

Faces red with wine and sweat, we wrapped our knees with newspaper
and knelt by the pile. We knew what to do, knew better
than to look: every breath a gasp now, Sister Kelleen drank,

drank and sobbed, while, heads bowed, we filled our skirts
with shards, large enough to have a good grip on them,
sharp enough to chafe a floor.


### 4. *Night Song*

A burning candle in one hand, a wine bottle in the other, she lit
every candle in the chapel. On the altar steps, on a blue and white
kitchen towel, her offering to us: a jug of milk, a rock of black chocolate,

a loaf of fresh brown bread. Next to it, we placed our alms to her:
a green, glittering heap of shards. We sat in a circle on the floor.
We ate. She drank. Then: *Now,* she ordered, *Now*—

and started singing. Kelleen, Kelleen drunk, tore
the cornet from her head, rolled black stockings
down her freckled legs, tied her hem to her waist—

and sang, loud and proud, she sang. And all night, to the rhythms
of her songs we scraped the chapel floor, shard in fist,
back and forth, back and forth, planing the boards,

Kelleen beside us, singing of whalers and sailors
    and faraway shores, of foghorns and luggers,
        and brothels and whores.

The more she sang,
    the deeper we scrubbed,
        and thick wood curls danced.


### 5. Crucifixion Dawn

And every year, at the hour the lapwings woke
behind the Chapel and night folded like a handkerchief
at St. Bosco's feet, she walked to the altar, faced the crucifix,

begged *Pie Jesu, tantus labor non sit cassus,* turned around,
and spat on the floor. Bowing our heads again,
we got off our knees, and went to her.

She held our heads to her belly, blessed us—a cross
thumbed on our lips, a kiss on our cheeks, whispering:
*Go. Pray for me. Pray.* Chased into silence, we stepped

across the impeccable floor, closed the chapel door,
then hushed it open to watch her take the cloth once more.
Watch how her face, legs, feet, wrapped in wine-soaked shrouds

shrank back into obeisance as she knelt by the altar,
unfolded the wings of her sleeves, and fell to the floor—
our Sister crucified: mouth, palms, belly against

the chafed, soft surface of her cross.

# The Radiator

Winters in Bruges were a monochrome
    of brown and gray, as were the huge
        wrought iron radiators of the nunnery.

I believed the banging North winds came
    to die in those pipes—I was eight then,
        ugly, awkward and shy.

Nuns slid along granite halls, hands
    in black tunnels of serge. Soon, dawn would cast
        its light through the stained-glass of the chancel.

I longed for that moment, when the hyacinth cape
    of the Virgin bloomed, and the cheeks of Jesus
        blushed as from a sinful dream.

My uniform itched. Knitted socks stopped
    an inch under the knee, flannel skirts
        half an inch above. My thighs were

chapped from rubbing on benches and stiff sheets.
    At 5:45, we stood at the Chapel doors,
        in shivering rows of three.

I was cold, always cold during those interminable
    Catholic winters. Mother Marguerite was late
        that day, and the radiator banged next to me.

I lifted my skirt, jumped, and straddled it –
    raw thighs against lukewarm metal.
        Annabelle pointed *I'll tell on you!*

Judith whispered *You'll be punished!*
    The door opened—I froze—like a mad
        magpie, Mother Superior's cornet

flapped in my face: *Get off there!*
    *Immediately!* she croaked.
        *Forgive me, Mother,* I dared, *but . . . why?*

Her knotted fingers were ice on my wrist.
    *It gives... ideas,* she said. I didn't look
        at the virgin's cape that day, or at Jesus blushing:

I couldn't figure out what Mother Superior meant.
    Years later, in the back of a black Peugeot,
        I understood: it was forbidden, hard, warm.

❊

# The Hour Between Dog and Wolf

Entre chien et loup: *time at dusk, when a wolf can be
mistaken for a dog.*

*I. The Good Ogre's Beard*

Home from the nuns once a month,
I run to his shack on the Wool Canal, climb
his belly to bury my face in the stir and curls
of his beard. Sun-bleached seaweed on his chest,
it purls, then stops by the slit in his vest
where he keeps his watch tied to a button
with string. On the left side of his head,
the funnel-shaped gash left by a German bullet.
*That Kraut's blood still shines on my bayonet,*
he smiles. I sit on his lap, on the wheezing
tides of his breath as his old fingers crochet
eel nets with green waxed flax—my head warm
between his forearms. In every knot he makes
I slip a wish: *Lord, save me from my family,
give me to him, may he live for ever and ever, Amen.*

*II. Herman the Bastard*

He died alone, Herman the Bastard,
in Bruges, during the long winter of '62, felled
and frozen next to his empty rabbit pen. I
never learned whose bastard he was, his name
taboo in our family: he was an atheist, read
banned books, drank beer and spoke
to Jews: *A sinner,* father barked.
But I escape to his shack on the Wool Canal,
while my family plays canasta and their claret
stains the tablecloth. I run to Herman,
waiting—huge—by his green enameled stove,

drinking beer, obese with life and stories.
*Ach ja, child, come, hurry,* he says, *the stories*
*are impatient, look, here they come!*
He points his finger to the door.

As in Holy Processions, they parade
into the shack: the silk-clad Dukes of Burgundy,
the pompous bishops of Spain, Rubens' peach-
hipped women and Emperor Charlemagne.
Bruegel guilds the air with country fairs and beer;
newly weds wave their bloodstained sheets
from somber windows at dawn . . .

Suddenly, swords clang, heads roll:
it's St. Bartholomew's night. In the guts
of steaming canals, Huguenot bodies
thump against barges filled with linen and lace.

*Ach ja, child,* he says, *humanity!*


### III. Feeding the Rabbits

He wraps his scarf around my neck:
*It's time to feed the rabbits, come.*
They rustle in the straw, the black male
chortles, the gray one scratches the trellis.
We kneel in his narrow vegetable patch, peel
leaves from cabbage, pull carrots, rutabaga,
leeks, both making believe we're not waiting
for the moment I long for, the one I fear
the best.

Then the church bells ring— and it happens
at last: like a mad, panicked dog, Herman
races through the garden, yelping *Quiet! No . . . Nooo!*
punches the air with his fists, crashes
into the rabbit pen: they squeal, I shriek, he
grabs around blindly, finds me, covers my ears
with his earth and cabbage hands:

*Run, run, the bells are howling, the catholic*
*wolves are hungry again!*
He picks me up, stumbles inside,

slams the latch and collapses in his chair, cursing.
  Later, as we eat raw herring
with bread dipped in beer, Herman shakes
his finger at me: *Remember, child:*
*don't listen to church bells—ever—*
*that howling will chew up your soul!*


IV. *The Hour Between Dog and Wolf*

  The roofs of Wool Row are charcoal
with dusk. *Ach child, look,* he says, *it's almost*
*the hour between dog and wolf: go now, go.*
  I pull away from his belly,
the shush of his beard, wave at him
hunched on the threshold of his shack,
  wave again before turning the corner,
but he looks away, afraid he'll call me
back, afraid I'll stay.
  I run through Bruges, through dusk
and sorrow rising from canals like black
mantillas and when—
  from the darkest side of the sky—
the vespers bells start howling:
I don't listen, I don't listen.

※

# Ladybugs

*Purulent psoriasis*, the doctor tells Sister Cecilia,
*calamine, and three tubs a day with linden extract.*
*She must stop scratching, and be a happier child.*

They put me in the infirmary. It's quiet there,
it smells of pigeons and mold. The zinc framed
attic windows leak. Now and then Sister Cecilia

coughs, lifts her eyes, sighs, then goes back
to cross-stitching "J.M.J."—for Jesus, Maria, Joseph—
on the convent's tablecloths, napkins and sheets.

She's frail, limps, and wears the brown habit
of the "Little Sisters of the Poor," the working nuns.
On the sixth day in the infirmary, my chemise and pillow

are dotted with red. *The ladybugs of suffering,*
says Sister Cecilia, *ladybugs on petals of pain.*
The chemise sticks to my skin, the million bugs sting,

bite, the rain needles the attic roof, drips
and slips into the linoleum cracks. I run to her, bury
my face in her lap. *Ach liebchen,* she sighs,

and—her old hands on my head—whispers:
*O Haupt voll Blut und Wunden, Voll Schmertz und voller Hohn;*
*O Haupt zu Spott gebunden, Mit deiner Dornenkron . . .*

She puts me in a bath—the linden flowers spin
like drowning bees—carefully detaches the chemise
from my skin, and strokes my cheeks, the Little Sister of the Poor,

on her knees and humming, she strokes my cheeks. Then:
*Liebchen, I have something that will help, but say*
*nothing about this: we can't own personal things.*

It's a round cardboard box, painted with tiny
white roses and gold leaves. Inside it, a pompon
of pink down and talcum powder smelling of lilies.

She lifts me from the tub, blots the water away with a sheet,
guides my hands to cover my eyes. I look through my fingers,
watch her bring the pompon to her lips, close her eyes

and kiss it. Like white solace, lily mist and *liebchens*,
*liebchens* cover my face and neck, back, buttocks and legs,
knees, ankles and toes. And for an instant,

I'm an angel so weightless she carries me—
*mein liebchen*—to my bed, pressing her painted
box to my chest as if to hold me down.

I think it was for her, for the nameless misery
of her life in that attic, and for the powder—
her panacea against absent mothers—

that I slept for days. So still, she said,
she put her hand to my heart to feel it beat,
Sister Cecilia of the Healing Pompon.

⌛

# The Pump

Every third Saturday after Mass, a nun strings
a train ticket on an elastic, slips it around my wrist, gives me
five francs and a licorice stick, and opens the convent gate
to the street. I walk down the cobblestones past the first corner,
then slip off my uniform socks and tie, run to the Gare du Nord
and board a brown train to Antwerp.

Beer-drinking soldiers play poker in second class cars.
In cadence with the rails—tick-a-*dak*, tick-a-tick,
tick-a-*dak*—I suck on my licorice stick, forehead against
the window, throwing spells on every crow and church I see.
In Antwerp, Platform 3 borders the zoo: it smells of
lions, urine and soot.

On the corner of Station Street, a red-haired woman
sells herrings and fries from a painted cart: Neptune,
laughing and pink, pinches a mermaid's nipple. Behind her,
seahorses fly into orange skies. I walk down Pelican Street,
hear Elvis Presley sing to Edith Piaf as café doors open
and close on sailors and high-heeled whores.

On Tram 5, I munch on herrings and fries as it clangs
past the Cathedral, past the harbor toward Grandfather's
house. Framed by leek and sorrel fields, it's a musty
brick place, hunched, somber. My mother and aunts
spend every summer there. They string rhubarb and skin eels,
chuckling in Walloon during gray kitchen afternoons.

I press my back to the wooden garden gate, squeak it
open, inch behind a row of yews and enter the greenhouse.
Shaking their white crosses like a hex, black spiders
escape into the purple shadows of concord grapes.
Garlic pompons nod at fat-bellied bees, mice shuffle
under the rusted dome of the inverted wheelbarrow:

I'm home. In a corner, a hand-pump, stiff
like a one-armed soldier, stands over a cement sink
encrusted with porcelain shards and seashells.
Next to it, a mess of jute sacks, crates and nets. I lift
a wooden pail, pour its fetid water into the pump's top—
it gurgles underground—I pull the handle up,

the pump burps out stale air, I push the handle
down, water gurgles, I pump faster: clear water
gushes, splashes, mounts. The seashells glisten
in the sink. I throw my uniform over the eel-nets,
untie my braids, step into the sink, pump again,
belly under the hard thrusts, kneel, and plunge my head

under water: I'm in the sea, in the sky, I'm a big-
breasted, winged siren. Eyes closed, arms open, I stand
in the sweet-anise air of the greenhouse. Elvis and Piaf sing
as Neptune, huge, laughing, wet, lifts me onto his shoulders.
Seahorses swing from my nipples, eels jive in my hair,
there is sun and music everywhere—we parade

through Belgium, trampling every convent, chapel,
church. Ships trumpet, trains hoot, sailors and whores
whirl in pagan processions. I wave at Brussels, blow
kisses to Antwerp freed, while—past the harbor roofs,
beyond the blond tides of Flemish wheat—clouds of crows
and crowds of nuns burn against orange horizons.

　

▨

# Chanel No. 5

One by one, my mother dips her Gauloises Bleues
    in Chanel No. 5, then puts them to dry on the table,
        on a blue handkerchief laced with flamenco dancers.

Later, she slips each cigarette in a silver case,
    checks her lipstick in the lid, smiles at it,
        and leaves the kitchen, humming to no one.

When the front door slams, I climb the counter
    and through the lace curtains watch her car
        wink   left,   left,   left—and leave.

At dawn, before my parents wake, I run to the garage
    at the far end of the garden, the cold sharp
        and gray like the gravel under my feet.

I open the heavy wooden door: a Dutch bicycle
    hangs from the ceiling, crates of onions, leeks
        and potatoes sprout against dank bricks.

Mother's '52 Fiat is linden green,
    with leather seats, a wooden steering wheel
        and Chanel lipsticks under the radio.

The ashtray is full of crushed Gauloises Bleues.
    I lift the bicycle from its hook, slip my hand
        under the mildewed saddle, and find

the matchbox I hide above the springs. A dancing
    red devil smiles at me from the lid, his horns
        black brackets against a Belgian flag.

I spit in my hands, carefully choose
    the least crooked butt, straighten it by slowly
        rolling it in my palms, up and down,

back and forth, put it between my lips,
   climb on the saddle—and light up.
      When I inhale the Gauloises Bleues,

mother and Chanel No. 5 fill my mouth, lungs,
   and scald them. I cough, cough, the nicotine
      makes me cry: I can finally cry.

And as I write *Maman* with my Gauloise
   in the indifferent air, I dredge up
      the longing for her from my throat—and spit.

&#9632;

# The Cellar

I want my father to stop sending me down there
to fetch his daily gin, and potatoes for supper.
But there's no saying no to him, and no more places to hide:
he's found them all. Outside, the cellar's rusted door
stains my hands as I yank it open, scraping a branch
that whips back, grabbing at me—like he does.

Six stairs stop by a second door, with a hasp
and a slit between two thick planks. I press my face to it,
whisper to the bottles and potatoes: *Go away, I'm coming!*
But how can they? We're all dammed in this big
brick house in Antwerp, and I'm the *Kapo*,
I have no choice: it's them or me.

I kneel in the cellar, pray: *Don't let me separate
families, don't let me kill a child* . . . then inch
toward the shelves—and reach. Sometimes
I think I hear a moan, a sob; sometimes it's a child's wail
so exactly like mine I think it comes out of me— so I quickly
put the thing back: *I'm sorry, I'm sorry.*

The worst are the potatoes. I know exactly
how they lived before, rooted deep in wild, salted polders,
where lapwings titter between cattails and winds,
where rows of loam run past the horizon—
and here they are now, uprooted and cluttered in crates,
limbs groping for a wedge of light from a cellar door.

But then, from up there, comes father's call, weary, irked,
with that pitch and threat in the last vowel of my name.
I grab the gin, the potatoes, hold them as far as I can from my body,
run up, throw them on the table, and escape to my room
where I stand pounding my ears with my fists so as not to hear
yet another cry for mercy.

*LOST SOULS ROAMING*

# Lost Souls Roaming

Driving through Nevada last June,
we watched tumbleweed bounce through heat-white
winds, whistling with emptiness. "Lost souls—
roaming" you said. I remember thinking how longing
runs through me, uproots, lifts, rushes until it
reaches you, or crashes into your absence
like tumbleweed against a fence.

January. We stand by the window,
watch snow scatter across the valley,
chased by high mountain winds. Is snow
the tumbleweed of winter? Is it a blizzard of souls
erring through summits and plains, searching
for the slightest fence, roof, rock—anything at all
to clutch—to stop spinning in the void?

# 7 A.M., a man and a woman

drive through Utah. They're silent;
his gaze somewhere between the hood
and horizon, hers almost hypnotized
by his hands on the wheel: how they were
not only his, but *theirs*, all night
in the Moving Rock Motel—its blue neon
buzzing Last Stop for the Next 100 Miles.
She tries to find words for their bodies'
naked blurs: those indefinable hues
of wrists, thighs, elbows—their tints and shadows.
Think of it, she wonders—
all the words there are for colors: cobalt,
rose, celadon, rust, saffron, blush, apricot,
gold. But words for human tones? Not
really olive or yellow, nor beige or brown,
not exactly gray, black or white.
They enter the desert—a blank on the map
slit by I-15, its red line flaring through heat—
and the landscape opens like a naked body,
trembles with skin-colored hills, bone-pale
rocks, coppery shadows and deep
crevices, dark. Everything around them
vague with nameless hues: all the shades
of skin, hair, nails—eyes even.
And yet, they drive on
as all the cars do, windows
closed, air
conditioned, impatient, un-
comfortable, her fingers
fiddling her flowered skirt, his eyes
fixed on asphalt, the yellow lines a code he reads,
hastening them out of that human-colored

emptiness where nothing grows, nothing
yields but the last cool shadows
the sun pulls back toward noon.

⌛

# Parentheses

Indiana. Noon. A man sits on a motel bed,
  wind blows in the tree outside his window
    in the branches, twigs and leaves,
    in the elm green shadows of the leaves.

On the walls and ceiling of the man's room,
  the tree's shadows breathe, wave with the wind.
    He sees arms in those curves,
    waving at him, reaching for something,

and parentheses too—that open and close around
  nothing. A shudder runs through him,
    through his shoulders and lungs,
    through his eyes and thoughts,

a shudder that makes him want to get up
  from his bed in the Indiana motel, (where
    he's in parentheses between
    Chicago and Bloomington

between his last love and the next,
  between selling fence-wire to the last hard-
    ware store and the next, between
    motels, between hopes), get up

from his bed in the Indiana motel and
  leave. Or close the curtains at least,
    those parentheses around a window
    he doesn't think of looking through—

and won't. Behind which there's Indiana,
  and noon, and an elm, with wind
    blowing through every branch,
    every twig, every single waving leaf.

# A Sunday Drive Through Eagle County

Near No Name, Colorado,
I thought I'd found a perfect poem:
lying by the side of the road,
a pregnant doe—frozen, neck
broken, legs open, the oblique
morning sun pushing her shadow
back to where she'd been hit.
    There was enough there
to write some twenty lines or so,
with metaphors shining
through the road-sign's bullet holes
and blood muddying up the last
patch of snow where she had been
run over. Not to mention
that Mahler's *Resurrection*
was wailing on the radio.
    But when the sun
struck another carcass, then
a buck's, then another one,
when my husband's knuckles
whitened on the steering wheel,
when we started counting, but
stopped after twenty three—
in less than as many miles—
when the Winnebagos we'd passed
passed us again with deer or eagle
silhouettes on their spare wheels,
when I said: *There's as many deer
splattered on the road as bugs
on the windshield,*
    I knew I'd lost it.

# In Pocatello

They kiss. His hand bobs in and out of her perm.
 She turns her head, looks at a green pickup go by.
  What are they, twenty, twenty-two?

They part. She crosses the street, rearranges
 her hair in the window of *Franky's First Class Trash*,
  turns the corner, hugging her faux-leather bag. And he

stands there, in his shapeless sweater and torn shoes,
 and I don't know what to think, what to feel
  when he doesn't move, doesn't go anywhere.

I want him to have a cat. A calico cat with a name like
 "Blake," his mother's picture on a brown TV,
  a family in Detroit. I want to slip into

his fingerprints, those crooked paths to him, the distant
 country of his body, an odor, a laugh, tell him
  to go to that woman, to find her again

on another dirty street corner, and open her
 mouth with a kiss that's angry now, hungry
  to suck out of her the numbness of Pocatello.

To speak a new tongue to her, the one he knows but
 never speaks, words from that world in him he keeps
  watching on TV, where oceans pound cliffs and carry

ships that leave, leave. To where I come from, and wait,
 and want him to stop standing on that mouse-gray
  piece of sidewalk that gnaws and gnaws at his soles.

# The Old Widow in Bruges

She sits by her window on Long Canal Row.
From under the rain's shuffle on umbrellas come
voices: hello, sad weather, yes. Good day . . .
It's Monday: her favorite day back then,
when *Madame's* chauffeur *Pierre*, knocked at her window,
tipping the cap of his bronze-buttoned uniform,
handing her the laundry baskets: *bonjour* Lily,
don't forget to starch *Monsieur's* shirts!
Sometimes he stayed, leaning against the door
smoking *Monsieur's* Turkish cigarettes, holding them
between thumb and index like Rudolf Valentino, and
humming to her as she undressed.
She went crazy when he left, mad
with lust and panic, hiding the soiled sheets,
tying her hair, catching her breath
before her husband returned from night fishing,
reeking of eels and ale. While he slept,
she sorted the laundry, smiling at *Madame's*
lacy things, stroking her cheeks with muslins
and silks, smooth as the chauffeur's
thighs around her neck . . .

Something lights Lily's old eyes—
she shudders, chases the cat from her lap,
pulls the pins from her hair, opens
the curtains, her window, her arms

to the rain.

# Plastic Beatitude

Our neighbors, the Pazzotis, live in a long
narrow canary-yellow house with Mrs. Pazzotti's old
father, their 2 daughters, *their* husbands, 4 kids,
a tortoise shell cat and a white poodle.
Their yard is my childhood dream: toys,
bicycles, tubs, bird cages, barbecues, planters, pails, tools
and garden sculptures: an orange squirrel eating a nut,
Mickey Mouse pushing a wheelbarrow, St. Joseph
carrying a lantern, his other blessing hand
broken at the wrist, and two tea-sipping toads
in an S-shaped love seat, smiling at each other
under a polka-dotted parasol.
On the yellow railing around the deck,
a procession of nine pinwheels. This May morning,
they thrash the air with each breeze like clumsy
angels nailed to their posts. On the garage wall
at the end of the yard an electric cord
shoots up to the roof. One half connects to a blue
neon insect electrocuter, the other half snakes to, then
disappears into a pedestal cemented on the cornice.
And there she stands, in plastic
beatitude—and six feet of it—the Madonna,
in her white robe and blue cape, arms
outstretched, blessing the Pazottis, their yard
and neighbors, lit from within day and night,
calling God's little insects to her shining light,
before sending them straight
to the zapper—tiny buzzing heretics
fried by the same power that lured them
to their last temptation.

# The Bumper-Sticker

"Yield" says the road-sign, so you do.
The bearded man nods thank-you, and passes,
*It's never too late to have a happy childhood!*
reads his bumper-sticker. You want to stop him,
ask if he knows how. No one waits for you at home,
so you follow: it could be God in that Dodge,
leading you to where you can change the past
like worn tires, or get a quick lube: the old stuff
dripping out murky and dark.

You'd get a new mother first: the pick
of the lot, a bright color—green maybe—
with safety features and a lifelong warranty.
A good reliable car, never running on empty,
with all kinds of options and lots of room
for both of you. You'd test-drive head high,
motor humming, gears changing noiselessly,
and never look back at the old jalopy that always
stalled and left you standing by the side of the road.

A new father next. He'd slide
into the passenger's seat and teach you how
to drive like a pro: check the rearview often,
and stop holding your foot on the brake fearing
you'll get in a wreck. He'd pull out
Technicolor maps, highlight the best itinerary:
*no dead-ends, no potholes, it'll be a smooth ride*
*my baby, tell me where you're heading*
*and I'll show you the way.*

The Dodge signals left. You follow, but
loose him in a tunnel when a sixteen-wheeler
reading *Safeway* passes so close it nearly
sends you to the wall.

# At the Musée Rodin in Paris

in front of a window
facing south, two white
marble hands fold
around air.
A label on the pedestal reads
*Le Secret.*
Did Rodin also sculpt
the air between those hands?
Is it caught there ever since:
the mold of secrecy?
    I waited hours for the sun
to flow through them.

    All it did was cast
a shadow to the ground.

# Hôtel des Touristes

She had nothing to fire her heart,
    he had a little house in the suburbs, so
        she married him, and tried to be fond of him.

She quietly gave him her days, the deceptive
    moans of her nights and raised her children,
        one by one, forgetting they were also his.

Every Sunday she visited her mother
    who rented chairs in the Parc du Luxembourg.
        She never missed a day in the leather shop,

making men's belts of calf: punch six holes,
    stitch the seams, sew the buckle, beeswax shine,
        control sticker three.

It happened around seven one morning
    in May, on the way to work. A gaunt
        North-African man sat next to her in the bus

and put his hand on her thigh. She didn't
    move or say a word but felt as if a sparrow
        fluttered in her chest.

She got down with him before her stop,
    waited on the sidewalk while he paid
        for a room at the Hôtel des Touristes.

There were lilies and ivy on the walls of room fifteen.
    She stared at them while he unbuttoned her blouse.
        His sweet smell, his dark and grainy skin

reminded her of calf—she touched it
    gently, first with the tip of her fingers, then
        with the back of her hand, kissed it,

and for hours begged: *encore, encore, merci.*
     Once, she cried: *Mon amour!* The voice
          startled her, she had never heard it so sweet.

He said *thank you* before he left.
     That winter, in bed, her husband smiled,
          said she bettered with age.

At Christmas, she gave him a book
     about Morocco and bought herself a nightdress:
          folds and folds of red silk.

# A Paris Blackbird

Along the Seine's left bank, near the Pont-Neuf, on the mansard roof
of my hotel, a scruffy blackbird squats by a chimney pot. Every day
for a week now, I have listened to him sing his April a cappella.

Not once has he repeated the same song, not once has he left
for the chestnut trees by the river, where he would have a better chance
of being heard, a better chance of enchanting some bronze-breasted female,

or lovers taking time off from noise. His song is all that counts.
It soars over roofs and terra-cotta chimneys, its trills cut by taxis,
cars and trucks coughing through the Parisian rush.

On the right bank of the Seine, three hours into Le Louvre's maze, past
Persian mosaics, glass-caged coins and Egyptian amulets, I slip
out of the tourist herd and head for a chair in a corner of the Greek Hall.

I sit there, shoeless, numb with knowledge and history, and stare at the bust
of an old woman, labeled *Anonymous, Greek, 11 BC*. She looks at me: weary,
terrible with banality, lips open, neck taut as if she were about to sing.

And as the crowds flock toward the Venus de Milo, nod at her beauty,
gawk at her perfect breasts, I look at this nameless woman, as I did
the scruffy blackbird—and listen for the cry caught in her bronze throat.

# Fountain in Avignon

Here, lovely retching moss-capped cherub: this penny's for you—
for all those copper prayers cast under your rippling chatter,
my penny's free of charge: spare change
for the cheap petitions flung into your stone depths.

No plea or prayer for this coin, I swear: this morning
is gratis, *pro Deo*. I no longer wish, nor pray—have entered
every chapel in this fervent city head high, heart free,
not giving a penny for candlesticks.

Under the Pont d'Avignon, I'll dance to cravings left
unanswered, to follies fulfilled, or dance for nothing.
At noon, when the sun swills every shadow from the streets
I'll make believe I believe in weightless hours, in fearless days,

for since that May dawn by an Antwerp fountain
in which I hurled everything I had—my faith—
hands in prayer under a spewing gargoyle, I asked only this:
    *Spare my son and daughter,*

then watched the rain slobber all it needed to
over the cathedral's stone-faced saints until the sun
etched them back again, black and vigilant in Antwerp's sky.
Since that morning I have wished for nothing,

and never will, so if I stroke your mossy cheeks whispering
sweet things, see nothing in this—but if my hands
happen to clench in prayer under your shallow babble,
throw them back, throw them out.

# Mortal Art

*to a friend in Chile*

Where you are, fall douses leaves and light—it's hard
    to imagine: everything here itches with green stubble,
days take their Provençal time to sink into dusk
    and the villagers are happy: they say the Mistral
left last week to 'die like a mad dog' in Italy,
    they can muse and gossip in the streets again.

The sky is aloof tonight, moonless. Shreds of cloud
    blotch the stars above Cézanne's mountain.
What wouldn't I give to have you here with us
    on this ordinary evening, to sit—albeit quietly—
in this resonant house, each of its windows facing
    the humble and colossal mount of Sainte Victoire.

That's how Cézanne spoke of Pissarro: *il est humble
et colossal*, as was his own ascetic path:
refusing to look beyond the monastic rampart of his canvas—
    *art is a religion*—shunning his mother's funeral
for fear of distraction, spurning the threat of an embrace—
    no girls, no jokes, no wine.

Is that what art demands? Relinquishment and exile?
    I can't endure such sullen habits, I want distraction,
need my gaze to waver, wild as moths on my window:
    how they hurl their wings against the glass!
Let me be fickle as the Mistral, lazy as Provençal lizards;
    give me the nuances of tenderness,

longing's appetites, the pagan buzz of sex—and may my art
    be mortal, nothing more than what it is:
a daily brush with grace. As for the last reckoning,
    I'm prepared, I know my answer by heart:

if art is a religion, so is desire's humble offering,
the pact of an embrace, a daydream's pardon, and

the crucial solace of missing a friend.

◰

*INVENTORY*

# Fallen

A friend had a Minnesota catalogue company
send me plant-them-yourself dahlias by mail.
The tubers nested in a rumpled mess of shredded paper.
One strip, caught deep in a root's cleavage
resisted, wouldn't come out. I pulled carefully
at the white paper, reading its truncated sentence:
*. . . enclosed manuscript for your Poetry Prize. I hope . . .*

I remembered those publishers' guidelines:
*we will recycle those manuscripts not selected
in a manner that will maintain the writers' privacy.*
Shredded, they sent the mess to nurseries, to protect
other bundles from being mishandled, torn. It took me
three hours to separate the fragments of that specific
font and paper from the other strips. I saved seven lines.

So this poem is for you—the one who wrote:
*blossom twigs in a glass jar by the bed* and *God of the hinge,
potential or fallen: it's that time of doubt again.*
I want you to know I love that line, its surrendering tone,
its rhythm—and pinned it to my wall. In Autumn,
when my first red dahlia blooms, I'll put it
in a glass jar, and place it under the word *fallen.*

# The Machinations of the Mind

The car crash we passed when I was five:
*drive on*, my father told my mother, *there's nothing
we can do*, as a woman spun in the fog like a shoeless,
aproned ballerina. She was young, had curly hair
and a spurting gash where her nose had been.
    Or how my father killed his Chesterfields,
gutted the stub until a worm of writhing
paper was left.
    Or how—from under an ex-
husband in Belgium—I'd count the slow,
red minutes on the TV clock across from our bed,
faking moans after less and less time . . .

Another sleepless night
sitting in the kitchen with my head in my hands.
Around me, the impeccable details of domesticity:
plates piled, spices placed alphabetically by the stove,
a spotless sink. There's nothing left to clean,
read, do, to conjure order, trash unwanted memories.

Outside, dawn's gray indolence, the color
of a screen gone blank after insomnia's *films noirs*,
all ending with the same image: a white-haired man
I saw years ago, on his knees in a blind-alley doorstep:
one hand endlessly waving his grief back into Antwerp's night,
the other hand stretched out to me—while a street cat
sharpened its claws against his chest.

Why is it we remember one thing rather than another?
There is no answer, is there? That beggar kneels in all of us—
drivers, moaners, fire-gutters, as we wave away
the selective machinations of our minds and *drive on*—
blast the radio, making believe we don't see
what spins and claws in our rearview mirrors.

# Loving You in Flemish

Let me love you in my tongue tonight,
heavy as Percheron hooves on fields
lying fallow and humming with rain,
their rich and dark loam steaming.

I know words lazy as canals
gliding among willows and yews,
green as Memling's velvets
or Bruegel's mossy farm roofs.

Angry clappers on Belfry bronze,
or moaning tugboat sirens, Flemish
undulates like dunes, or glistens
with the spume of granite piers at Ostend.

Taste my tongue— a salty shrimp—
bitter with chocolate and beer:
the Trappist ale is naughty, the Devil ale
is sweet like cream over sorrel and eels.

I know the lingo of the blue Antwerp alleys
where women lust from the sea—they're
too hungry for one sailor only . . .
Let me love you with words uttered

only there, words the many-tongued
whores whisper, listen:

> *Kom mee oengze nacht in Antwaarpe verdwoale,*
> *Mokt de klank van de stroaten a' ziel amoureus?*
> *Al edde gien geld oem plezier te betoale*
> *'k zen 'n goe vrake, iel lief en genereus*

Oengder de glans van de moanestroale
Word iel oengze wereld een uuwelaksbed
Kom mee nor bordiele vol vrawen en matroezen
Verget awe noam en al de rest . . .

# English Flavors

I love to lick English the way I licked the hard
round licorice sticks the Belgian nuns gave me for six
good conduct points on Sundays after mass.

Love it when 'plethora', 'indolence', 'damask',
or my new word: 'lasciviousness,' stain my tongue,
thicken my saliva, sweet as those sticks—black

and slick with every lick it took to make daggers
out of them: sticky spikes I brandished straight up
to the ebony crucifix in the dorm, with the pride

of a child more often punished than praised.
'Amuck,' 'awkward,' or 'knuckles,' have jaw-
breaker flavors; there's honey in 'hunter's moon,'

hot pepper in 'hunk,' and 'mellifluous' has aromas
of almonds and milk. Those tastes of recompense
still bittersweet today as I roll, bend and shape

English in my mouth, repeating its syllables
like acts of contrition, then sticking out my new tongue—
flavored and sharp—to the ambiguities of meaning.

Ⅺ

# Taxi

Boston high-rises are glued
to the night, alleys soaked with cardboard rain.
"It's very mild for the season" barks
the taxi-driver. I almost tell him how
moist your voice was, how your thighs,
and voice and skin urged my *more, more ,
again, again.*
    A truck unloads on Oak Street,
baskets of oysters, boxes of trout,
rain bouncing off sidewalks so hard
it seems to rain up. The window wipers
wave faster now, *every thump-squeak-
thump-squeak* scoring the distance between us,
*good-bye-good-bye.* Logan nears,
blurs, nears,
    a skycap yanks the door open:
*What's your final destination, lady?*
    I give him five bucks,
my bag is heavy and ripped.

# Letter from Jake's Place, Durango

Dear B,

I know the big lady won't come to clear the table,
she's leaning over the bar, arms buried under tired breasts,
talking to a biker. I push the plates away, grits and tepid beer.
This place is thick with dust. I'll stay here, it's a good place,
dark enough to forgive myself: I long for home again.

This time for a rainless summer day in Antwerp,
seagulls yacking at tugboats pulling ships back to port.
The Scheldt swells with the North Sea tides: sweet waters
mingle with salt. An egret slips its neck into that thickness,
gobbles an eel and rises: a ripple, a crease in the sky.

Not a ripple in the river though, only summer waves
so languorous you can actually feel them suck up and come
down again, licking hulls and banks slick with mussels.
I long to watch your hand dip into cones of newspaper
greasy with *fritches*, then grab raw herrings by the tail

and swallow them whole. My lips are heavy
with Flemish: the guttural sounds of the lowlands.
Take me away from this sidewalk café—hurry!—
we'll book a room with a view of the Scheldt and leave
the windows open. Wide open.

# Unable to find

the right way to get out of bed,
we watch the shades cut dawn
into thin slices, waver a while,
shoulder to shoulder, then join, lazy.

Let's leave this room now: it's given us
all it can, let's go—it's Sunday—have
breakfast out, find a table for two: two eggs,
two toast, two coffees—black. No, nothing

plain: latté. We'll read the paper,
the story of a man who rescued the only thing
he wanted from the rubble of his collapsed shack:
his cat—and be moved by it, and like that;

or play hangman on our paper napkins,
find easy words—no double-meanings: day,
night, rivers . . . then send the game to its fate,
crumpled on our empty plates.

Let's step inside a church, sit through a wedding,
a christening, a mass for the dead, but leave
before the last *amen*. We'll take the long way home,
make plans for summer—winter even.

# This Morning, God

Four A.M. Snow on the roof like a stone slab.
I wake in the dark again, leave my husband,
tiptoe into the kitchen, silently stir my coffee
with a plastic spoon: I don't want to wake him.

I won't forget those dawns without him:
slam the doors, slap the lights on, stir in my coffee
with metal things to chase away the ghouls
of the lonely choking me in their burlap wings.

Today, I stand in the middle of our house,
everything still with unblemished intensity: no wind,
no moon, not even the weary whir of an insect hovering.
Leave me here: with the smell of coffee, and this

other scent ebbing from my body: sex, my husband,
our bed. Let me tiptoe through our house, press my palms
and face to the bedroom door an instant so the rest of the day
will be easy: work, phone, traffic, more work –

the incessant beating in my chest for two now.

# After a Noisy Night

The man I love enters the kitchen
with a groan, he just
woke up, his hair a Rorschach test.
A minty kiss, a hand
on my neck, coffee, two percent milk,
microwave. He collapses
on a chair, stunned with sleep,
yawns, groans again, complains
about his dry sinuses and crusted nose.
I want to tell him how
much he slept, how well,
the cacophony of his snoring
pumping in long wheezes
and throttles—the debacle
of rhythm—hours erratic
with staccati of pants and puffs,
crescendi of gulps, chokes,
pectoral sputters and spits.
But the microwave goes *ding!*
A short little *ding!*—sharp
as a guillotine—loud enough to stop
my words from killing the moment.
And during the few seconds
it takes the man I love
to open the microwave, stir,
sip and sit there staring
at his mug, I remember the vows
I made to my pillows, to fate
and God: I'll stop eating licorice,
become a blonde, a lumberjack,
a Catholic, *anything,*
but bring a man to me:

so I go to him: *Sorry, honey,*
*sorry you had such a rough night,*
hold his gray head against my heart
and kiss him, kiss him.

# Zen

The drop caught
        in the curl behind your left ear lobe
                swells, quivers and
        falls
—a tiny pear on your shoulder blade—
        stops,
takes on the color of adobe,
        of hay,
                rolls

                        down

                                sideways,
speeds along the inverted crescent of the scapula,
        along the brief tension of a muscle—
                or is it a tendon?—
                        (you're shaving, every surface of your back moves)
then
        slows
down,
                ambling         along   your   spine,

and, because I'm looking only
        at that minute transparency,
                I shiver when it suddenly
        sucks up another drop,
plumps,
        swells,
                ovals,
                        and quavers now,
buxom and boorish toward your loins.

Can't you feel it? Doesn't it tickle, tease
                as it leaks
        to the left,
                then lasciviously
stretches where your buttock rounds, firms, and . . .

oh, now,
        quick, before it
slips
        into the moist fold by your leg—
           I crouch and catch it
with the hard,
      upcurled
         tip of my tongue.

# August

We are alone again,
    children and friends have come
        and gone, a hush of sage

wafts through the air,
    I sew a button to your shirt,
        it's August – placid, fair.

You're writing in your room,
    looking up now and then
        to stare at the nasturtium

and lavender I planted by the gate,
    for their gold and purple thrusts,
        their sedulous reaching,

and when I bring your old
    frayed shirt to my lips,
        cutting the thread with my teeth,

I hold it there simply
    because it is yours, and has
        our smell, familiar and common.

I press the denim against my face,
    tasting the air in it, the sun,
        and realize how light it is,

how easily it could slip
    out of my hands, out of this moment—
        how the smallest distraction,

the slightest inattention
    could leave me here alone,
        with nothing but my face in my hands.

+ diligent,
painstaking

# So it's today

and in the chokecherry this year:
    the first leaves turn ugly, there—
        by the open gate.

I grab the sweater you left on a chair,
    wrap it around my shoulders, and—
        as I did for days last year until

I couldn't keep up with the season—
    I pick every rusting leaf from the bush,
        each wrinkled thing from our yard

and crush them in my apron pocket.
    It's a simple gift for you—for us—
        such an easy thing to do

for a few more days of summer.

                            ⌧

# Migration in Red

I bring in the geraniums. A season
caught in pots: a red parade on the windowsill.
With hummingbirds hidden in their wings,
geese point their arrows south. From garden
to kitchen, I huddle another migration
against my breast, touch each flower,
breathe in summer from every bloom.
I hesitate, but finally bring in the vulgar
hibiscus sent by an ex-lover during
midsummer's heat. The garden
      is empty. It's that time again:
all the reds inside reaching for the last,
insouciant rays behind the window's muslin,
their sanguine fists, like mine, raised against winter.

# White-Out

Storms slam the hill, fists of ice cuff the house fifty,
sixty times a day. Gale after white gale grind a branch
deep against the roof's skylight, drawing a dark 'Y'
on the glass. I say it aloud—and hear *Why?*

It's because of El Niño, says the radio, El Niño
who messed up air masses somewhere above the Pacific
months ago. And I think of the boy I drove past at dusk,
kicking a snow bank as he waited for the bus, red cap

over black eyes, shrugging, angry at something that
hurt that day, so he let the snow have it: cursed it, punched it,
kicked it, one furious foot after the other, until the bluff
shattered at his feet. How the inexorable happens:

a snow bank trampled for a yes or a no, a *Why*
stuck between me and the sky for months to come because
air masses were mangled over an ocean last spring.
White, white: buried or blowing: everything's white—

I'm going mad with winter: even God could
get lost on a night like this, searching for shelter,
for something unshattered—while, sheathed in ice,
twigs click at my walls with their fortune-telling tongues.

⌛

# The Syllables of Longing

White-out. Black ice on the road.
A snowplow blinks its last spinning
blues before leaving the valley. No one
left on the road but us. You say you've
had it with winter, you're ready for spring.
I'm not. I don't miss the glossy
spread of leaves on twigs and trees,
those greens oozing from everything,
and fat bugs coupled in flight . . .
     I'll never tire of snow, the quiet
pollen of winter: watch it lift, waft, twirl
and settle, fitting so utterly into itself,
like words in age-old prayers:
those relentless syllables of longing.

# From My Window, I See Mountains

The morgue man pulls my father out of wall C:
the drawer so heavy he must brace his foot
against another one to pull it open. It jams
halfway, this is how far it will go: one half
available for viewing, the other no.

A voice cries out in the anteroom, then turns
into a wail so unbearable the morgue man leaves.
I'm alone with my father again. This time, I
lift the sheet further than allowed, and look.
This time, it is he who is frozen. And I see his

rage, down there, dark—like a fist
crammed between his legs. I touch his hands, the huge
Dutch hands that almost killed me, almost killed
my daughter, but once—on a shore in The Hague—
built me a sand castle, the morning after

his mother's funeral. It took him all day,
the deepest terror I remember, watching him
build that castle with the odd tenderness of brutes,
stroking the sand with weightless hands while I
sat at a distance, not knowing what to think,

what to do, Dutch rain sprinkling the sands
like a blessing. When the castle was done, he raised
moats around it, and mountains circling them,
while dusk wrapped us in its cerements, then night.
Not a word was uttered, even when we climbed the dunes

back to his mother's house, where I watched him
rock her wooden shoes in his lap, a hand in each
battered thing, the kitchen stove sighing.
After I buried him next to her, I flew back to this new
country, to this house surrounded by mountains,

with mountains around them. Some days, they seem
so quiet, so unchangeable, I think: shock, fissure, fault;
I want: chasm, quake, wave. But pray: plant me here
a while longer, plant this in me deep: nothing's perpetual,
eternity is only a word – kind as consolation, but as brief.

# Inventory

Thanksgiving today. Soaked with sleet.
No sun for six days—six is the Devil's number.
I have looked through this window,
at these American skies for two times six years.
My wall is covered with photographs of distant friends.

This is my third garden. The first two blossomed in Belgium.
Where there is no Thanksgiving. Where my father is buried.
Where I was raised and raped and worked. Where I had five lovers,
but loved only one. Where I gave birth to three children.
A blond son, a dead daughter, a blond daughter.

Shadows grew in my first garden. Two larches in my second.
Because of North sea winds and how they stood, they fused
into one trunk. It wounded them at first, that rubbing together—
the frailest larch loosing sap for months, a lucid sap that glued them
to each other at last. I saw it as an omen for my life.

I give thanks for the lowlands in Belgium.
For Flanders, her canals and taciturn skies. For the tall ships
on the river Scheldt. For coal pyramids in Wallonia.
For the color of hop, and the hop-pickers' songs.
For Antwerp's whores who woo sailors in six different tongues.

Six is the Devil's number. My grandfather and a farmer
killed six German soldiers and threw them in a Flemish moor.
I can no longer give thanks for that: I ask mercy.
Before I die, I'll plant a larch by the moor—*miserere*—
the soldiers' mothers will never know it was done.

I prayed six times for the death of my Jew-hating father,
I ask mercy for that also: it's Thanksgiving today.
I give thanks for my son and daughter, for the man I love
who taught me a new language.
For this garden's life and sleet.

Before I left for this vast continent,
I stole sand from the river Scheldt,
an inch of barbed wire from a Concentration Camp near Antwerp,
a leaf from the chestnut tree behind Apollinaire's grave,
but no weed, not a seed of it, growing from my father's ashes.

In Belgium, the day is almost over.
Soon, a new century will make History: *miserere.*
Four larches grow in my garden: one for my son, one for my daughter—
and far from a moor in Flanders, the other two fuse
here: in America. In America.

# NOTES

"The Worlds in This World" is for Mathieu;
"The Feather at Breendonck" is for Eleanor Wilner;
"Leek Street" is for Jay Schneiders;
"Amen" is for Carol Houck Smith;
"Little Sisters of Love and Misery" is for Brigit Pegeen Kelly;
"The Radiator" is for James Anderson;
"The Hour Between Dog and Wolf" is for Maëlle;
"Ladybugs" is for Renate Wood;
"The Pump" is for Maureen;
"The Cellar" is for Len Roberts;
"Plastic Beatitude" is for Thomas Lux;
"At the Musée Rodin in Paris" is for Herman de Coninck;
"Mortal Art" is for Stephen Dobyns;
"White-Out" is for Aidan O'Brien;
and all the love poems for you, Kurt.

Page 30: in "Little Sisters of Love and Misery": *"Pie Jesu, tantus labor non sit cassus"* is Latin for "Jesus blessed, let not in vain such labor be."

Page 39: in "Ladybugs": *O Haupt voll Blut und Wunden, Voll Schmertz und voller Hohn; / O Haupt zu Spott gebunden, Mit deiner Dornenkron!"* is German for "O head of blood and wounds, for sorrow and scoffing born, / O head wreathed for mockery, with your crown of thorns!" (*St. Matthew Passion*— J.S. Bach, Libretto by Picander).

Page 63: in "Mortal Art": The phrases "the threat of an embrace" and "no jokes, no girls, no wine" were shamelessly stolen from "Cézanne's Success" and "Cézanne's Coldness"—both poems by Stephen Dobyns.

Pages 69–70: in "Loving You in Flemish": The Flemish verses are a loose adaptation from a song by Wannes van de Velde.

> Let's lose our night together in Antwerp,
> Don't the sounds of the street seduce your soul?
> And though you're too broke to pay for pleasure,
> I'll be your woman, generous and sweet.
>
> Under the glimmering rays of the moon

The whole world will be our bridal bed
Come with me to brothels full of women and sailors,
Forget your name and all the rest . . .

Page 73: in "Letter from Jake's Place, Durango": "Fritches" are Belgian potato
fingers fried in suet.

# ACKNOWLEDGMENTS

My sincere thanks to the editors of the following publications in which some of these poems or earlier versions of them first appeared:

*Atlanta Review:* "The Syllables of Longing";
*The Bellingham Review:* "In Pocatello";
*Denver Quarterly:* "Days of Rules," "At the Musée Rodin in Paris";
*Harvard Review:* "White-Out";
*Hayden's Ferry Review:* "Amen," "Hôtel des Touristes," "The Radiator", "Little Sisters of Love and Misery";
*i.e. magazine:* "English Flavors";
*International Quarterly:* "Leek Street," "The Hour Between Dog and Wolf"
*Kalliope:* "Zen";
*Many Mountains Moving:* "The Pallor of Survival," "From My Window, I See Mountains," "Sunday Drive Through Eagle County";
*Marlboro Review:* "7 A.M., a man and a woman";
*Maryland Poetry Review:* "Chanel No. 5";
*Massachusetts Review:* "The Cellar," "Loving You in Flemish," "The Worlds in This World," "Inventory";
*Negative Capability:* "After a Noisy Night";
*Nimrod:* "Amen," "Letter from Jake's Place, Durango";
*Ploughshares:* "The Feather at Breendonck";
*Salamander:* "The Old Widow in Bruges";
*The Spoon River Poetry Review:* "A Paris Blackbird," "Ladybugs";
*The Sycamore Review:* "Unable to Find the Right Way".

"The Bumper-Sticker" was included in *Drive, They Said: Poems about Americans and their Cars* (Milkweed Editions, 1994);
"Migration in Red" in *Each in Her Own Way* (Queen of Swords Press, 1993);
"August" "From My Window, I See Mountains" were included in *The Writing Path* (Iowa Press, 1995);
"The Bumper-Sticker," "The Cellar," "From My Window, I See Mountains" in *Writing Our Way Out of the Dark* (Queen of Swords Press, 1995);
"Letter from Jake's Place, Durango" and "Parentheses" in *Night Out: Poems about Hotels, Motels, Restaurants and Bars* (Milkweed Editions, 1997);
"So it's today" was included in *A Poem A Day* (Steerforth Press, 1996);
"English Flavors" won First prize at the 1996 National Poetry Contest.

I was extremely fortunate to work with Stephen Dobyns, Carol Frost, Brigit Pegeen Kelly, Thomas Lux, and Renate Wood at the Warren Wilson MFA Program for Writers—thanks to Ellen Bryant Voigt, John Skoyles and Peter Turchi.

*Merci de tout mon coeur*, Charles Simic.

To you, my American friends—*to each one* of you—for including me in the family and for your unconditional patience, faith, love, humor and bounteousness: thank you.

Friendship and gratitude to Steve Huff, Thom Ward and Bob Blake, and love to *ma* Bobo, my Maureen, The Amazing Hip, the BOA girls, The Lugubrious Sex Pretzels, *ma* Spunk et *mon* Bro—and such nostalgia for Larry Levis and Al Poulin.

# ABOUT THE AUTHOR

A native of Belgium, Laure-Anne Bosselaar has lived throughout Europe and the United States. Fluent in four languages, she has worked for Belgian and Luxembourg radio and television stations, published a collection of French poems, *Artemis*, and is currently translating contemporary American poetry into French, and Flemish poetry into English. She holds a Master of Fine Arts degree from the Warren Wilson Program for Writers, and now resides in Cambridge, Massachusetts.

⊠

# BOA EDITIONS, LTD.

## NEW POETS OF AMERICA SERIES

Vol. 1    *Cedarhome*
          Poems by Barton Sutter
          Foreword by W.D. Snodgrass

Vol. 2    *Beast Is a Wolf with Brown Fire*
          Poems by Barry Wallenstein
          Foreword by M.L. Rosenthal

Vol. 3    *Along the Dark Shore*
          Poems by Edward Byrne
          Foreword by John Ashbery

Vol. 4    *Anchor Dragging*
          Poems by Anthony Piccione
          Foreword by Archibald MacLeish

Vol. 5    *Eggs in the Lake*
          Poems by Daniela Gioseffi
          Foreword by John Logan

Vol. 6    *Moving the House*
          Poems by Ingrid Wendt
          Foreword by William Stafford

Vol. 7    *Whomp and Moonshiver*
          Poems by Thomas Whitbread
          Foreword by Richard Wilbur

Vol. 8    *Where We Live*
          Poems by Peter Makuck
          Foreword by Louis Simpson

Vol. 9    *Rose*
          Poems by Li-Young Lee
          Foreword by Gerald Stern

Vol. 10   *Genesis*
          Poems by Emanuel di Pasquale
          Foreword by X.J. Kennedy

Vol. 11   *Borders*
          Poems by Mary Crow
          Foreword by David Ignatow

Vol. 12   *Awake*
          Poems by Dorianne Laux
          Foreword by Philip Levine

Vol. 13   *Hurricane Walk*
          Poems by Diann Blakely Shoaf
          Foreword by William Matthews

⌧